What the ____ Do You Really Want?

Marc Sims

What the ____ Do You Really Want?

Marc Sims

© 2006

Cogent Media

1803 W. 95th Street

Chicago, IL, 60643

Cogent Books

P.O. Box 5415

Chicago, IL. 60680

CogentMedia@yahoo.com

Marsha Johnson
Editor

Special Thanks To:

Karen January

Corey Mays Foundation

Ranoule Tatum

"The Motivators Motivator"

Lady Oshun

The Temple of Divine Esoteric Teaching Center

Erica Wise

Holistic Health Consultant

Marsha Johnson

All My Family and Friends in Chicago

Introduction..............................9

Habits. 17

Window of Opportunity.............25

Sixth Sense............................33

Moments of truth.....................41

How to Win.............................49

Poverty Consciousness...........59

No More Excuses..........…………69

Today you can choose to move forward or backwards.

Today you can choose to feel unloved, disrespected, and unworthy, or you can choose to value and love yourself.

Today you can choose to be held up by fear and resentment or you can decide to some take action toward your goals and win!

Ask yourself:

What do I want?

What is stopping me from getting what I want?

What am I afraid of?

What do I believe?

Introduction

The purpose of this book is to help you focus on your goals and your purpose in life. This book will help you clear your mind so you can focus on completing your daily goals.

If you are reading this, it's evident that you want a more abundant life and want to achieve all of your goals as soon as possible.

You can begin the process of achieving your goals today, but you need to believe in yourself and the source of your power.

Why are you reading this self-help book? What are you looking for? Are you looking for an easy, painless way to become a millionaire? Are you looking for an easy, painless way to lose twenty-five pounds? Are you looking for an easy, painless way to find someone to love you the way you want to be loved?

Here is the question: "what do I really want?" Answer: "I want to love being me. I want to become a loving, unselfish, and nonjudgmental person. I want to endow the world with peace and enlightenment by being peaceful and enlightened."

You can do this if would are willing to commit your life to this mission. You can fulfill your true potential if you really want to make a serious commitment. You really can "have it all" but you must be grateful for what you have now.

The modern mind is cluttered with so much "stuff", it is hard to focus the mind beyond the concept of surviving. The average person's goals are food, clothing, shelter, and personal pleasure.

You may consider yourself an "average" person, but you want to know how to become an above average person. You want to know how can you attract and obtain all the money, love, and peace of mind you feel you deserve.

You will begin to get everything you want when you focus on achieving goals that will benefit other people as well as yourself.

Take a hard look at the multimillionaires you see on television.

They are serving the masses with goods, services, and entertainment.

There is no secret to success! There is no magical method that will make you instantly successful! There is only hard work! There are only hard choices! If you don't choose to excel, you choose to remain average.

There is nothing wrong with being an "average" person if you are happy with your simple life.

The average person already has everything he or she wants. If they really wanted a more abundant life, they would have worked harder or smarter to obtain their desires.

In order to achieve your goals, you will need either a very strong drive for success or a very intense dissatisfaction with your current status in life. Average people are very comfortable and content with their average life. Their job pays them a livable wage. Their home is sufficient and their neighborhood is bearable. Their life is relatively good. If this sounds like you, put this book down and enjoy the rest of your day.

This book for the person who is ready to transform their life. This book for the person who is ready to rise to new levels of success.

What is stopping you from getting everything you want?

Are you a lazy and extremely disorganized person? Are you a chronic procrastinator? Are you a proactive person or a reactive person? Are you a loser or are you a winner?

It is time for you to get over the dysfunctional parts of your childhood and grow up! It is time for you to accept your failures and boldly face your current challenges! It is time for you stop blaming your family, friends, or modern day capitalism for your lack of success.

Maybe there was a time you could blame "the system", "the Man", or forces beyond your control for your underachievement. Maybe your fourth grade teacher or some other authority figure crushed your self-image. However, you are not a small child anymore. That was then, and this is now! This is the moment where you say, "Yes, I can!" This is the moment when you finally take responsibility for the rest of your life! In this moment you begin the process of winning!

Habits

Is today the day you become a millionaire?

Will you become a millionaire tomorrow, next week, next month, or next year?

How will you become a millionaire? Will you become a millionaire in one day by winning the lottery? Will some billionaire feel sorry for you and give you a million dollars?

Think realistically! For most people, making a million dollars takes a lot of time. It may take years and years of preparation for you to become a prosperous athlete, entertainer, or businessperson.

Some people become millionaires by saving and investing a small percentage their money for ten, twenty, or thirty years. Most people would love to become a millionaire, but the odds are totally against them.

Would you be happier if you were a multimillionaire? Would this kind of prosperity "change" you? Would you be a nicer person or become a very arrogant person? Would you become a more loving and caring person if you had a few million dollars? What kind of person are   you now?

Do you believe your habits reflect your personality, and if you develop the habits of a multimillionaire or any other successful person, will you finally end your paycheck-to-paycheck, average lifestyle? Do you have realistic and detailed plans for getting everything you want?

What you are attempting to do is to obtain higher levels of success. You are attempting to change your life for the better. You want to develop a new way of life. This new life you want to achieve may not be much different than your life now, but you will enjoy it more. You want more freedom to be you! You want to be free from or at least enjoy your job, and to reduce your bills. You want to be free from people who do not understand you. You want the freedom to create, to cure, to comfort.

You want to know, "how do I become this great and wonderful person?". One way you can change your life is to create some new habits.

You may have habits of watching too much TV, talking on the telephone, or surfing the Internet. You may have the habit of misplacing things, and wind up wasting valuable time looking for lost items. Your life may be totally disorganized and thus, you spend too much time trying to get things in order yet you accomplish little.

Your bad habits could be a reflection of your scattered thoughts.   You want it all, but you know you can't have it both ways! You are conflicted!

Are you like the person who fights against the establishment but wants to be recognized by the establishment? This person wants to change the world, but they have trouble focusing their attention on changing themselves. They want to be wealthy without the responsibilities of being a multimillionaire. They are wishful thinkers and habitual procrastinators. They have trouble changing their bad habits that were established during their childhood.

It is time for you to replace your old habits with new habits that will move you closer to your goals.

Start today by reducing the amount of TV you watch! You can start a new writing habit by writing one new page of your book or life journal for the next seven days. You can start a book reading habit by reading for a minimum of five minutes everyday.

You can start a new eating habit by consuming less sugar, dairy, and carbohydrates.

The most important habit is the habit of writing down your goals for each day.

You can write this list of top priorities before you go to bed or immediately when you wake up. Keep the list with you at all times and read it many times during the day. The list will help you focus on establishing new, good habits and focusing on your goals.

But how do you turn away from old ways? Bad habits can be very rewarding! They give a temporary feeling of peace and comfort. Bad habits produce bad thoughts and our bad thoughts result in bad choices. A set of new positive habits will lift you above your current level of comfort.

However leaving a comfort zone can be very painful. The thought of eating less, exercising more, and investing 10% or more of your income can hurt! Singing in public, speaking to groups, or writing a book that will be critiqued by your peers is very frightening!

You may need to seek some professional help to change your behavior. There are psychiatrists, hypnotists, spiritual advisers, and life coaches who can help you turn your new habits into a way of life. There are also herbal supplements and vitamins that can help you focus your brain on achieving your goals.

Habits are established slowly, one hour at a time, one day at a time. The habits that will make you successful will take time to develop. This sounds corny and trite, but it must be repeated: There Is No Overnight Success.

Achieving success takes a lot of time, but developing the habit of doing the things when they are supposed to be done will speed up the process of reaching success.

Window of Opportunity

Time does not wait for you or anyone else!

The clock is ticking and your time is running out! If you are a paycheck-to-paycheck commoner, you only have a few minutes in each day to work on achieving your goals.

Each day, there is a window of opportunity for you to take some action that will move you closer to your goals. This window may open for only a few minutes in the morning, afternoon, or evening.

When you are confronted with a moment of truth you must decide whether to move forward or fall behind. You must decide to take action toward your goals or waste valuable time participating in an instantly gratifying activity.

This is your choice! You are basically on your own! Rich people have a staff of personal and professional assistants. They don't have to clean the toilet, cut the grass, or complete any other mundane task. The rich and successful also have secretaries, nannies, or lackeys to do the things they do not have the time to inclination to do. The rich and very successful can clearly focus their attention on manifesting their daily goals. You may have little or no support, and face a million distractions everyday.

You intend to do so much more than you actually get done.

Yesterday went by so fast, last week was a blur, and last month was just as obscure as the past ten years.

You can't go back to last week or ten years ago, for those windows of opportunity are closed forever!

A child star has a five to ten year window of opportunity. A would-be teen idol has even fewer opportunities. The careers of some entertainers did not blossom until they were in their twenties or thirties. Some opportunities appear quickly, and some opportunities are years away.

An athlete has to prepare five to ten years before they are ever confronted with their window of opportunity.

A young athlete will hone his or her skills for ten to fifteen years, all the while knowing that the big money and professional stardom may only last five to ten years.

Losers ask themselves: "Why should I spend years preparing myself for one or two big opportunities? Why should I exhort enormous amounts of time and effort with no guarantee of success? Why should I endure numerous failures and embarrassments just to experience only a few years of great success?"

Dreaming or talking about how you are going to be successful is so easy and painless. Actually doing the hard work can be mentally painful! The thought of being a failure is potentially heartbreaking and embarrassing. However, if you want to win, you must prepare yourself for your windows of opportunity.

Daily preparation is essential for great success. Accomplishing small goals are preludes to achieving great success. Completing each day's tasks builds momentum and establishes good habits.

Imagine you are a boxer preparing for a big nationally televised fight. If you win this boxing match, you will be promoted to a multimillion-dollar prizefight.

You have three months to train for the big contest. You have to lose fifteen pounds. So your goal is to lose five pounds for each of the next three months and to win the big challenge.

Your first step is to develop a training routine. The next step is to discipline yourself to focus on your goals and follow your new routine. There is no guarantee you will win, but the possibility of winning increases each day you prepare yourself to win. You may not get another opportunity like this, so your determination has to be intense!

Focusing on your purpose for winning will keep you from straying away from your diet and exercise routine. Your burning desire will give you the power to prevail over your daily moments of truth; to eat or not to eat? To exercise or not to exercise? To work your plan or to play, watch TV, or talk on the telephone? These are your moments of decision.

These are the moments to prove to yourself that you are finally serious about winning.

You move closer to achieving your goals, one meal at a time and one exercise routine at a time!

Remember, your time is running out! You are getting older by the minute! Your windows of opportunity are closing! Take at least one small step each day and move closer to your goal. If a window of opportunity is about to close, you will have to choose: give up or break through!

Sixth Sense

Where do your thoughts come from? Do they come from "God" or do they come from you? Or do they come from the inherent intelligence that resides in every atom? These infinite electrical impulses are invisible. Billions of atoms traverse through your body. You are these atoms and these atoms are you. The source of these powerful atoms is all around you. You can choose to connect to these pulses of energy or you can choose to ignore them.

It does not matter from where you think your thoughts originate; it is only important that you believe in the power of your thoughts. It is important that you believe in the source of your thoughts.

Most people believe "God" is a being that is in control of the universe, including the six billion human beings currently living on the planet Earth.

Whether God is a spirit, a being, or the intelligence that is in every atom, human beings have to make choices. You can let the "spirit" move you or you can choose to move in the opposite direction of your feelings.

You have the power to choose, but your choices are sometimes directed by your intellect and other times strongly influenced by your emotions.

Some decisions can be pondered upon, and some decisions must be made instantly.

For instance, you are driving and in the distance you see a fork in the road. You must make a quick decision. Should you make a right or a left?

The different choices flash in your brain and you only have seconds to make the correct choice. If you make the wrong choice you could drive into a traffic jam or a dead end. The wrong choice can cause a traffic accident. Your decision is a thought, and in less than one second, that electrical pulse activates your brain, nervous system, and your muscles.

Everyone has to make life-changing decisions.

Should I go to college? Should I drop out of college? Should I get married? Should I stay married or get a divorce? Should I continue to work a dead end job or start my own business? Should I save and invest a small percentage of my income or continue to live paycheck to paycheck? Should I remain in this house, this city, this state or should I move and start a new life? Should I participate in a relationship that could result in an unwanted pregnancy, sexually transmitted disease or heartbreak, or should I spend another Friday night alone?

One decision can launch your life into an orbit of desperation and regret. Just one decision can extend your life or can shorten your life. You cannot prolong the inevitable forever. You must decide!

No one can make the best decision in every situation, but you must consider the causes, the effects, and the consequences of your decisions.

Earth's gravity is a very strong force, and so are the forces of irrational fear, superstition, and religious dogma. All these extremely strong forces influence your decisions.

You have made some good decisions in the past and it is time for you the make choices that will move you to higher levels of success. Your life is a long from being over, and you have more   big decisions to make.

You have the power to achieve your goals but you do not want to experience the pain of making the wrong decision. You have searched outside of your self for some magical resolution to your problems. You have read motivational books and listened to motivational recordings over and over and over again. You have sought the guidance of clergymen, spiritual advisers, psychics, astrologers, and motivational gurus. You have gained much knowledge and wisdom but at times you remain indecisive. You have yet to reach your true potential.

Is there such a thing as a sixth sense or is the sixth sense just common sense? If you believe you have a sixth sense, use it to make quick decisions. Connect to the source of your power and make the correct choice! A calm and clear consciousness is the key to making the best decisions.

A calm and clear mind is also a personal choice. Tap into the intelligence and power that is within you and all around you.

Moments of Truth

Every day, you encounter moments of truth. This is where you face all your inner demons, fears and self-doubts. This is where you put up or shut up! This is where you fail or prevail.

The questions are: should you eat or not eat? Should you complete your homework assignments or should you go outside and play? Should you spend your money foolishly or save and invest your money for financial independence? Should you constantly criticize other people and complain how they are making your life miserable or should you work on improving yourself? Should you forgive yourself and your enemies or should you continue to hate and condemn those who have harmed you?

Most motivational books basically say the same thing in slightly different ways. You have read these books and you know what you should be doing, and you know how, when, and why you should do the things necessary for great success.

However, when you are confronted with a moment of truth, you take the path of least resistance. You take the easy way out.

You choose instant gratification over long-term success. You voluntarily choose ultimate failure for the feelings of short – term success. Your emotions win out over your intellect. Once again, the weakest parts of your character are revealed.

Eating large amounts of food is instantly more rewarding than exercising or meditating. Starting a habit of exercise and meditation is hard physical and mental work.

Asking someone to buy your product or service can be extremely frightening. Asking someone special for a date can be unnerving. Watching TV for hours is so easy and painless. It is very hard to break a life long habit of procrastination via mindless TV viewing.

For many people, delaying real, success driven gratification is a way of life. Procrastination is a part of their daily routine. Real success or failure is too much for them to handle. Deep in their subconscious, there are thoughts of inferiority and unworthiness.

You are attempting to "self-help" your way to success. You know you should be able to do this but you have not yet achieved your major goals. If great success seems almost impossible to achieve, you may need to seek professional help.

You may need an "intervention"! You may need to face the possibility that you have been in deep denial for years! You may need to go deep into the subconscious parts of your mind and accept the bad parts of your life and embrace your future with a positive attitude of gratitude.

Your happiness, your billion-dollar life style, and everything else that you want are all inside you. Maybe you should seek first the kingdom of heaven that is within you. Then you can really appreciate who you are and your current station in life.

You already have everything you need but you want more because you think these material "things" will make you a happier person.

Remember, life is full of paradoxes. So you could begin to manifest all the physical things you want after you address your spiritual, and emotional needs.

You are full of fear and you procrastinate because you no do not believe in you.

OK! You think, "My self-image, my self-concept, my self-esteem is not strong enough to endure the pain of rejection, failure, and embarrassment". You ask yourself, "What am I afraid of? How do I love myself and believe in myself to the point where I'm fearless?".

You can improve your self-image slowly or quickly – it's up to you. You can dive into the deep part of the pool or first wade in the shallow part. You can take a ride on the tallest roller coaster or first get on the kiddy one. You can make your first public speech in front of a corporate audience or speak to grammar school students. You can make your first sales presentation all by yourself or go on sale calls with a seasoned sales champion.

Most people should start slowly in the process of heightening their self-images. Focus on the fact that improving your self-image and defeating your fears and inner demons is a process.

The process of transformation could take nine days or nine months. In nine months a cell transforms into a full-term infant. In nine months, a child goes from the fourth grade to the fifth grade. It is amazing to see humans, plants, and animals develop in a deliberate period of time. You can have a transformed life, a more abundant life, by the end of next week!

As a human adult, your self-development is a choice you make everyday. So when you are now faced with your daily moments of truth, remember, you can instantly muster some positive energy, take action and win. Just focus on what you want, and why you want it!

Your daily moments of truth are a test of your character. Your daily moments of truth challenge your core beliefs.

How To Win

Winners seem to have out of body experiences. They go into a zone and go with the flow. The zone is clear and free of mental debris. No thoughts of childhood horrors. No mean adults, no grammar schools embarrassments, no feelings of neglect, and no conscious or subconscious fears. For a few moments everyday winners clear their minds and directly connect to the infinite intelligence that surrounds all of us.

The subconscious minds of losers and underachievers are full of fear and resentment, jealousy and poverty. Consciously or subconsciously, these individuals may not have gotten over the rotten parts of their childhood. Those old experiences have shaped their characters and limited their beliefs. Losers and underachievers do not believe they can have a more abundant life.

All things are possible, but first, you must truly believe all things are possible!

There was a time when people thought man could not go beyond the Earth's atmosphere. There was the belief that the earth was flat, and the sun revolved around the earth. Man's thinking has changed from millennium to millennium. Mankind has progressed more in the past few hundred years than in the previous two thousand. The collective consciousness of human beings has expanded. You only need to believe in the source of your power. Only believe!

Remember, Dorothy had the ruby slippers, but she did not know she could have gone back to Kansas at anytime. You could have been a greater success in life but do not completely believe that you already have the power to achieve all of your goals.

Who you are and everything you have are reflections of your thoughts. Your thoughts are a sum total of your life experiences, including your education.

Your personality and temperament were formed during your childhood. You are also a creature of your habits. Every action you take and every decision you make reveal your character.

You already know this, but you continue to wait on some supernatural event that will make you extremely successful.

Everything is real! The Earth, every atom in the universe, and all your thoughts are absolutely real!

To become "successful" you need desire, plus effort, plus time. An intense desire is necessary for a dramatic transformation. It will take a tremendous amount of effort to get everything you want. It will also take some time to get everything you want! You do not become rich, famous, thin, healthy, and fearless over night. Success takes time, so use your time wisely.

It is time for you to have a breakthrough! Change can happen in an instant. Or you, at least, can begin the process of transformation instantly. Start by intensely believing you are worthy and powerful!

How do you get what you really want? First, write down your goals, your purpose, and your mission in life. Then write a plan of action for today, this week, and this month. Finally, go sit down in a comfortable chair or sofa. Sit quietly and clear your mind of any negative thoughts of fear, resentment, jealousy or poverty.

The inner mind cannot distinguish between a real or imagined event. So imagine having everything you want. Visualize your negative thoughts, your fears, and your habit of procrastinating fading away. Also, fill your mind with images of you being your best and winning! Next, spend a few minutes imagining your self-image being energized by billions of brightly colored atoms.

These visualizations will give you the mental strength to be proactive and change your life. You may not have to totally alter your personality, but you must change something about your behavior to get everything you want.

Change is inevitable! The planet earth and your physical body are constantly changing. Losers resist change because they do not want to learn and grow. Some losers believe they are not smart or strong enough to win. Some people are comfortable losing, so stay away from contagious losers and underachievers. Losing and underachieving have become their identity. Subconsciously, they believe their character and their self-image are unchangeable. Their life stories are filled with bad choices that reflect their recurring thoughts of unworthiness and powerlessness. What do losers think about? Losers sometimes think about winning but they lose because they do not believe they can win.

Criminals think about crime. Educators think about educating.

Winners think about winning! Believe you can win! Only believe!

You are reading this book because you want to rise to greater levels of success. You may have a desire to go all the way to the top. The way to the top begins with small steps, one step at a time.

Small steps will lead you to small successes. Over time, your small successes will evolve into big successes. However, you must not allow a setback to defeat you. You must continue to move forward and persevere!

Your windows of opportunity are closing. Soon you will be faced with final moments of truth. Trust your sixth sense and be proactive.

Poverty Consciousness

Do you hope for the best, but expect the worst?

Are you the kind of person that wants something for nothing?

Do you take much more than you give?

If so, you may suffer from a poverty consciousness.

Someone with a poverty consciousness lives in fear! They live in fear of abandonment, homelessness, starvation, loneliness, or some other negative but conceivable notion.

Selfish and irrational thoughts cloud their minds. "If I give away some of my food I will go hungry. "If I give away my clothes I will become naked." "If I give away some of my hard earned money I could become poor." "If I give someone my money or my valuable time, what will I get it in return?" "If I give, how long will it take before I receive my money back tenfold?" "Who is going to give me some of their money?" "If I give, give, give, how will I get it back?" "Who is going to help me get what I want?"

You may already have everything you want but you don't see it! A poverty consciousness or a prosperity consciousness is a reflection of one's self-image.

Poverty is a state of mind. Prosperity is a state of mind. Some people have everything they need but they really do not enjoy what they have. Some have everything they want but are not really happy with themselves. Some people want to know how to get everything they want but do not want to do what is necessary to fulfill their desires.

Some people are unapologetically selfish and are in deep denial about their selfishness. This characteristic is partly a reflection of their poverty consciousness. It ruins personal relationships and businesses relationships. Many marriages would have never ended in divorce if one or both partners weren't so selfish. Sometimes there is no give and take in a relationship because one or both partners do not know what they really want. They don't know themselves and don't want to face the reality of an evolving relationship. One or both partners will not even consider giving their love, their time, or anything else until they first get what they want. One or both partners are so selfish they demand more than their partner can actually give. Their selfishness attaches conditional strings on anything they give. Unfortunately, some people are almost incapable of giving unconditionally. They don't know how nor do they want to know how to become a loving person.

If you don't have everything you want, it could be because you refuse to change your attitude, your habits, and your behavior.

Changing your behavior, habits, and beliefs may take weeks, months, or years of personal development.

Ending a poverty consciousness is a paradoxical process.

If you want more prosperity, give 5% or 10% of your income to some worthy charities. If you want more money, begin to spend less money and live below your means. Save and invest 5, 10 15, 20% of your income. Invest in stocks, bonds, gold, silver or your own business. Invest in yourself and go back to school.

A lot of people have trouble doing this. Just the thought of living off of 95, 90, or 85 percent of their income is painful. The thought of reading books on creating wealth or running a successful small business are exhausting. Thoughts of being poor, homeless, or hungry are just as exhausting. Anyone who does not really believe in him or herself can be defeated by these thoughts.

You cannot avoid facing all of your fears. You cannot avoid the inevitable forever! Soon or later you will have to face all your fears. Everything you think you want is on the other side of all your fears.

Remember your childhood fears? The playground thugs, a mean grammar school teacher, or some other vicious adult?

Eventually you had to confront these fears, and although they were painful realities, you survived. But the pain left an indelible impression on your brain.

Grow up! That stuff happened years ago!

Today is a new day. Tomorrow will be a new day. You are not really fearful of the future - you just choose to invest in your old fears!

If you have 10% of your earnings electronically taken out of your check and put into a mutual fund you will not be stricken with unbearable pain. If you donate a few dollars to a worthy charity, you will not be stricken with unbearable pain.

If you have a poverty consciousness, a money journal can help you replace your perception of lack with a prosperity consciousness. You can begin to get all the money you want when you start accounting for and appreciating all of the money you have now.

Start today by writing down where you spend your money, how much money you spend each day, and why you spend your money.

This journal will help you see that you have all the money you need.

This journal will also help you see that prosperity is much more than money!

If it is too painful or you are too lazy to start a money journal, you should realize that you just ain't ready for real prosperity! If you continue to think thoughts of lack, you will not be able to attract all the prosperity you want.

No More Excuses

What happened? What made you snap?

What made you shy, selfish, or fearful?

Who crushed your ambition?

Was there a series of traumatic experiences during your childhood or adolescence?

When you were an infant, your every need was provided. You had no responsibilities. As you grew older, more responsibility was given. You had to begin taking care of yourself. Each responsibility was a shock!

"What", you say, "I have to bathe and clothe myself?" "I must clean my room?" "I have to do all these other chores around the house?"

As a child, many of the hard choices were made for you. As time progressed, you began to make the hard choices of life.

Some people make the transformation from adolescence

to an adult successfully. Some people do not, and have many mental

wounds from the experience.

To get all the things you want, you will have to replace your limiting beliefs and become a slightly different person. Before this transformation takes place you need to make an honest evaluation of yourself.

Do you really see yourself realistically? Or do other people see you better than you see yourself? Are you ready for some deep introspection, and are you ready to accept an intervention?

It is time for you to deicide to take responsibility for the rest of your life. If you feel you do not have the mental ability to do so, get some bona fide professional help! Do not feel embarrassed that you cannot become "successful" all by yourself.

Make the decision to align yourself with positive individuals like a mentor, a life coach, or some other extremely wise person that will help you achieve your goals!

Changing your beliefs or truly believing in yourself is mental journey. The first step of this journey can be overwhelming because it is natural to focus on the thousands of connecting steps. Just focus on taking a few steps everyday! Just focus on what you really want!

You say you know what you really want but do you want to know how

get it? How to overcome years of laziness, fear, self-doubt, low self-esteem, and the habit of procrastinating? How to get the energy to leave your current orbit of a passionless life?

Do you ask, "How do I renew my mind and transform my life?" "How

do I replace my negative beliefs with positive beliefs?" "How do I

trust God or better yet, "how do I trust the God in me?"

Some people already know how to get everything they want, but their fear of hard work keeps them from developing any persistence. You are afraid of days, months and years of hard work. Do you wish, hope, and pray that you will supernaturally get everything you want?

You want the things you want because you think these "things" will make you happy. You want tangible things because you believe they will give you the feelings of success.

You cannot touch a feeling. A feeling is like spirit. You cannot see a spirit or a feeling. You just think you can. Spirits and feelings are in the mind of the beholder. Some people can watch the same movie and feel differently about it. Some people are emotionally inspired by a particular selection music, a particular religious service, or a particular political rally.

Different people are inspired by different things, at different times. What inspires you, and why don't you use this particular person, place, or thing to inspire you to transform your life?

Does the "spirit" move you, or do you move your spirit? What do you really believe? Do you really believe there is a God, or a "higher power"? Or do you believe you are a god? Some people believe in God but they don't believe in themselves. They are "ye of little faith".

Shame on you if you believe in God and you feel unworthy to have a more abundant life!

Shame on you if you say you believe in a higher power and have yet to transform your life!

Shame on you for reading self-help books and listen to self-help recordings and continue to be an underachiever!

Shame on you if you have thoughts of hate, envy, or condemnation!

Your spirit, your feelings, your nervous system, your belief system, your mind and your body are all one.

This is it! Your life ain't no movie! All the things you want are not going to magically appear.

Your desire, your passion, your drive, your goals, your purpose will get you the things that you want!

You can instantly begin the process to rid yourself of self-doubt, laziness, fear, and procrastination. These feelings are habitual choices. Replace these feelings by continuously focusing on your goals, your purpose, and your passion!

Say out loud, "I believe in myself!"

Say out loud, "I believe in the source of my power!"

"I believe in myself!"

"I believe in the source of my power!"

Fear no more and make no more excuses, for now you truly believe in yourself and the source of your power!

Dear Friend:

What you really want is inside you!

Take at lest one minute out of each day to connect to the power this is inside you and all round you.

Just sit and be silent!

In these moments you connect to the source of your power. Use theses moments of consciousness to intensify your desires for a better life or intensify your dissatisfaction with your current life.

Choose to let go of any resentment, envy, or fear.

In this silent moment, all your fears and self-doubt disappear.

The fear, procrastination, hate, anger, and any other debilitating emotions were just thoughts. It's all thought! It is all your thoughts.

In this silent moment of thought, choose to create peace, prosperity, miracles, and anything else you want.

Take at lest one minute out of each day to love being you.

I wish you peace and prosperity.

Marc Sims

P.S.

Develop the habit of replacing a negative thought with a positive thought. **Develop the habit of taking action rather than procrastinating.**

Focus on what you want. Focus on what you believe. Focus on the divinity that is within you.